THE SHEPHERD IN THE CLASSROOM

How Teachers Lead, Guide, and Protect the Flock

By

Dennard Mitchell

The Shepherd in the Classroom

Printed in the United States of America

979-8-234-06764-7

NL Publishing

Dedication

To every teacher who has ever wondered if the work matters.
To those who stay late, show up early, and lead with heart.
To the shepherds who walk ahead so others can find their way.

This book is for you.

Your work is sacred.
Your impact is eternal.
Thank you for leading the flock.

Table of Contents

Introduction:

There is an image as old as time. A shepherd, steady and quiet, moving through rough terrain with a flock in tow. Not leading for applause. Not guarding for recognition. But because someone has to go first. Because someone has to care enough to protect the vulnerable, guide the lost, and create a path where there was not one before.

Teachers, you are the shepherds of our time.

You do not just stand at the front of the room. You walk ahead into emotional storms, academic gaps, behavioral struggles, and life changing stories that students carry in their backpacks alongside their books. You are navigators of trauma. Builders of belonging. First responders to confusion and crisis.

This book was written for you. Not to add another theory or checklist to your plate, but to remind you of what you already are: a powerful, irreplaceable force for good.

Each chapter draws a parallel between the ancient role of the shepherd and the sacred, everyday work of the teacher. Through real life stories, practical insights, and powerful truths, you will be reminded of the impact you make. Not just when students achieve high marks, but when they show up uncertain and leave feeling seen.

You will find yourself in these pages.

You will rediscover your purpose when you have lost it.
You will regain your footing when the path becomes steep.
And most importantly, you will realize that you are not alone.

This is a love letter to the overlooked.
A rally cry for the weary.
And a mirror for the heroic.

Because being a shepherd does not require a title or a pedestal.

It requires the courage to keep showing up with love, with vision, and with the unwavering belief that every student is worth the journey.

Part I: The Call to Lead

Chapter 1: Leading the Way

The Shepherd's Role

Out in the open fields, the terrain is unpredictable. A sheep herder's job is not just to follow the flock. It is to lead it. They scout the safest paths, steer clear of cliffs, and guide their sheep toward water, food, and shelter. The sheep do not always know where to go or what dangers lie ahead, but the shepherd does. The shepherd walks first.

A shepherd does not lead with noise or fear. They lead with presence and consistency. The flock follows not because it is forced, but because it trusts.

This kind of leadership is quiet but firm. It is intentional yet flexible. A shepherd must be deeply attuned to both the individual and the collective needs of the flock. They must understand the rhythms of the land, the patterns of the sky, and the subtle cues of change in the air. This awareness is not developed overnight. It comes through years of commitment and careful observation. The shepherd stays out in front because they have already assessed what lies ahead. They lead not only with vision, but with wisdom.

In times of danger, the flock looks not to each other, but to the shepherd. The sheep know who to trust because they have seen their shepherd navigate storms before. They have watched them move steadily through dark valleys and guide them into the light. It is not the loudest shepherd who gains their trust. It is the one who shows up day after day, even when the sky turns dark.

The Teacher's Role

Classrooms are also filled with unpredictable terrain. Each school year presents new obstacles such as academic pressures, family instability, social media distractions, peer conflicts, trauma, and uncertainty about the future.

Teachers, like shepherds, go ahead of their students emotionally, mentally, and practically so their students can safely follow.

Teachers lead with their example. They show leadership in how they speak, how they show up each day, how they respond to frustration, and how they recover from failure. In many cases, a teacher is the first safe adult a child encounters who models calm in chaos and purpose in uncertainty.

Just as sheep can sense confidence and calm in their shepherd, students can sense when a teacher truly cares and when that teacher is walking ahead with purpose.

Students do not just absorb curriculum. They absorb posture. They notice the tone in your voice, the consistency of your presence, and the way you carry both authority and compassion. A teacher who leads with integrity sets the emotional climate for the classroom. The way you handle interruptions, discipline, praise, and mistakes is not just about maintaining control. It is about building trust.

Being out front does not mean being unreachable. In fact, the most effective teacher leaders are present. They are on the floor helping during group work, at the door greeting students by name, and in the hallway encouraging a shy student to keep going. They are not distant. They are invested.

Sometimes leadership looks like innovation. A teacher who introduces a new way to learn math or brings literature to life through role play is creating a path where none existed. Sometimes leadership looks like sacrifice, such as staying late to rewrite a lesson or calling home because a student has been absent too long. Sometimes it looks like quiet endurance, showing up the next day even after the hardest one.

A teacher leads by demonstrating what is possible. They go first in courage, resilience, and listening. They become a map that students begin to trust.

The Weight of Leadership

It is important to acknowledge the emotional toll that comes with leading. Just as a shepherd carries responsibility for the entire flock, a teacher often carries the invisible weight of each student's story. There is the student who stays after class to share a family struggle, the one who hides anxiety behind sarcasm, and the one who always says they are fine while their eyes tell a different story.

This kind of leadership requires both strength and softness. A leader without empathy can become rigid. A leader without boundaries can burn out. Teachers must learn to lead with open hearts and protected energy, pouring into their students while also refilling their own capacity.

Even with the challenges, the reward of leading the way is unmatched. When a student begins to believe in themselves because you believed first, when they finally understand a concept they once feared, or when they begin to dream bigger because you introduced them to a new possibility, that is the gift of going first. You create a path they never knew existed.

Real Life Example: The Teacher Who Paved the Way

At a high school in rural South Carolina, there was a student named Mason. His father had left when he was young, and his mother worked night shifts. He was barely passing and often skipped school. Most adults had already given up on him. Some said he was too far gone. But one teacher, Mrs. Alvarez, saw something different.

She noticed he liked to sketch during class. Instead of correcting him, she said, "These are really good. Have you ever thought about architecture?" It was the first time anyone had asked him about his future.

Over the next few weeks, she helped him research colleges, meet with the guidance counselor, and even arrange a tour at a local community college. After that, he showed up every day just to sit in her class.

Years later, Mason returned. He was now a licensed architect. He handed Mrs. Alvarez a blueprint of a small house he had designed. At the bottom of the page, he wrote, "For the first person who showed me a way forward."

Additional Example: Leading from the Margins

Ms. Desai taught in an inner city middle school in Toronto. Her classroom included students from more than twelve countries. Many were learning English, and some had only recently arrived. She did not share a common language with all of them, but she led with clarity, patience, and joy.

Each Monday, she began class with a world map. One student each week placed a pin on their family's country of origin and shared a cultural tradition. At first, students were hesitant. By the middle of the year, they were proud and excited, teaching their classmates dances, words, and recipes.

Her leadership made inclusion visible. She led from the front not by forcing assimilation, but by creating belonging. In that environment, students followed not because they had to, but because they felt seen.

Leading the Way Through Change

Education is constantly evolving with new standards, shifting expectations, and emerging technologies. To lead in the classroom is also to be a learner. Teachers often lead through changes they did not choose, which requires staying grounded in core values while adapting to new realities.

Leadership today may include trauma informed practices, social emotional learning, and advocacy for mental health. It may involve speaking up for students whose needs are overlooked or addressing issues that others avoid. Teachers lead not only in instruction, but also in culture, policy, and change.

The Invisible Leadership

Some of the most powerful forms of leadership are never recognized publicly. You do not need a title to lead. You do not need attention. Every time you give a struggling student a fresh start, support a colleague, or choose what is right instead of what is easy, you are leading.

Leadership in education is often quiet, but it is deeply transformative.

Reflective Takeaway

Leading the way does not always mean having all the answers. Sometimes it simply means being the one who steps forward first and says, "You can follow me. I am here for you."

Teachers are trailblazers not for recognition, but because they understand that behind them is a generation that needs guidance and trust.

You lead when you care. You lead when you persevere. You lead when you believe in every student and the future they can create.

Your leadership matters.

And it begins each day when you choose to walk ahead.

Reflection

Where in my classroom am I currently walking ahead of my students?

How do I model resilience when lessons do not go as planned?

Do my students follow me because they have to, or because they trust me?

What visible behaviors communicate calm leadership?

What invisible habits shape my credibility?

Discussion Prompt for Teams

How does our school define leadership beyond titles?

Research Anchor

Educational research on instructional leadership shows that teacher clarity and credibility significantly impact student achievement (Hattie, 2018, Visible Learning).

Chapter 2: Knowing the Flock

The Shepherd's Role

Shepherds do not simply watch over sheep. They know them. Each sheep may look similar from a distance, but a good shepherd learns to tell them apart. One limps slightly from an old injury. Another has a habit of wandering. A third becomes anxious in open fields. Shepherding well requires attention to small details, subtle differences, and needs that are not immediately obvious.

To know the flock is to move beyond surface level observation. It means noticing who hangs back when the group moves forward, who eats less, and who needs extra attention. The shepherd develops an understanding of each animal's temperament, habits, and vulnerabilities.

This deep familiarity allows the shepherd to lead effectively. It is not about control. It is about connection. When sheep hear the shepherd's voice, they follow because they recognize it. They recognize not just the sound, but the one who has fed them, led them, and protected them.

Knowing the flock builds trust, and trust creates movement. A flock that feels understood is easier to lead.

The Teacher's Role

In the classroom, knowing the flock means knowing your students, not just by name or grade, but as individuals with identities, needs, and stories.

This begins with intentional presence. It is the difference between calling on a student by a general description and saying, "Marcus, I remember you mentioned your grandmother is in the hospital. How is she doing?" It means taking time to ask questions, observe interactions, and listen not only to what students say, but how they say it.

Students are not data points. They are complex individuals living full lives beyond the classroom. Knowing the flock means paying attention to who is thriving, who is struggling, and who is simply trying to make it through the day.

Sometimes this understanding comes through conversation. Other times it comes through quiet observation. The student who stops raising their hand, the one whose laughter fades over time, or the one who keeps their head down are all communicating something. Effective teachers read these signals the way shepherds read the sky.

To truly know your students is to create space for authenticity. It is building an environment where students can be seen without feeling the need to perform.

Creating Systems for Knowing

Knowing a classroom full of students is not easy, especially with busy schedules and large class sizes. That is why intentional systems matter.

Some teachers use student surveys at the beginning of the year that go beyond favorite subjects and explore family life, goals, and challenges. Others schedule regular individual conferences or use journals where students can communicate weekly. Some keep notes after class, recording small observations such as a student appearing tired, smiling more than usual, or lingering after dismissal.

Technology can support this work. Digital tools can track engagement, assignments, and progress, but they should never replace the human connection. Data can guide awareness, but empathy must guide action.

Knowing your students also means advocating for them. When a student has an individualized education plan, a 504 plan, or an unmet need, a teacher who truly knows that student does not allow those needs to be overlooked. They speak up, take action, and ensure support is provided.

Real Life Example: The Note Card System

Ms. Greene, a seventh grade English teacher, developed a simple but powerful system. On the first day of school, she gave each student an index card and asked them to respond to four questions:

What is something you enjoy doing outside of school?

What is something you wish adults understood about students?

Who is one adult in your life you trust?

What is one thing that makes school challenging for you?

That evening, she reviewed the cards and created a spreadsheet with notes. Each week, she selected five students to check in with through a quick conversation, a follow up question, or a comment about their interests. It took only a few minutes each day.

Over time, she noticed a shift. Students opened up more quickly, asked for help more often, and began to see her not just as a teacher, but as someone who genuinely cared.

Knowing the Flock in Times of Crisis

The importance of knowing your students becomes even more critical during times of crisis. When students experience trauma such as loss, displacement, or community disruption, their behavior often changes. They may withdraw, act out, or become silent.

A teacher who truly knows their students will notice these changes and respond with compassion rather than punishment. Instead of asking, “What is wrong with you?” they ask, “What is going on, and how can I help?”

Trauma informed teaching is not about excusing behavior. It is about understanding its root. A shepherd does not punish a frightened sheep. They move closer. The same is true for teachers who lead with empathy.

Beyond Academic Knowing

Knowing your flock also means understanding what inspires them. What excites them, what frustrates them, and what they dream about.

It is easy to focus on grades and behavior, but knowing the whole child includes recognizing their joy. Some teachers use music to connect by inviting students to share songs that represent them. Others offer choice in projects so students can express learning in ways that reflect their strengths.

When students feel known beyond academics, they begin to trust the learning process itself.

Knowing the flock means giving students the opportunity to be more than learners. It means helping them be seen as human beings.

Additional Example: A Breakthrough with Jayla

Mr. Thompson had a student named Jayla who rarely spoke. She often submitted work late or not at all. He tried multiple strategies, including changing her seat, offering encouragement, and contacting home, but nothing seemed to work.

One afternoon after school, he noticed Jayla sitting alone on the steps. Instead of leaving, he sat beside her.

"You do not have to talk," he said. "But I will sit with you if you would like."

She nodded, and they sat in silence for ten minutes.

The next day, she turned in her assignment. A week later, she stayed after class to ask for help. Gradually, her walls came down. Jayla did not need a solution. She needed to know she was not invisible.

Reflective Takeaway

To teach well is to know well.

Knowing your students takes time, attention, and emotional investment. However, the impact is powerful. A student who feels known is more likely to take academic risks, ask for help, and believe they belong.

Shepherds do not wait until sheep are in crisis to notice them. They know their flock so well that they can prevent danger before it arises. Teachers who know their students can do the same.

Know your flock not just to lead them, but to care for them.

Because being known may be the first step in a student believing they matter.

Reflection

Which student in my class do I know the least about?

What systems help me intentionally learn student stories?

How do I distinguish behavior from underlying need?

What assumptions might I be making?

Discussion Prompt

How does our school ensure every student is known by at least one adult?

Research Anchor

Belonging is strongly linked to academic persistence and motivation (Walton and Cohen, 2011).

Chapter 3:
Protecting the Vulnerable

The Shepherd's Role

Within every flock, there are always sheep who are more vulnerable than the rest. It may be a newborn lamb with unsteady legs, an older sheep slowed by injury, or one that naturally lags behind. A good shepherd does not overlook these differences. They anticipate them. They slow their pace when necessary, remain alert while others rest, and gently guide those who drift too close to danger.

Protection is not passive. It requires constant awareness. Shepherds scan the horizon for threats such as predators, storms, and unsafe terrain. They respond before harm reaches the flock. They remain attentive to the wellbeing of the group, especially those who cannot yet advocate for themselves.

At times, protection means standing between the flock and danger. At other times, it means carrying the weakest sheep through difficult terrain. Often, it requires sacrificing personal comfort to ensure the safety of others.

The Teacher's Role

In the classroom, vulnerable students are not always easy to identify. Some are quiet and withdrawn, while others hide their vulnerability through defiance or humor. Some carry trauma, while others face learning differences, mental health challenges, poverty, neglect, or language barriers. A teacher, like a shepherd, must be both observant and compassionate, ready to protect in ways that are both visible and unseen.

Protecting students goes beyond physical safety. It includes emotional, mental, and psychological wellbeing. It means creating a classroom where every student feels safe to show up as they are, without fear of shame, and with the confidence that they will be supported.

Seeing What Others Miss

Vulnerability in students often appears in subtle ways. It may look like declining participation, sudden changes in mood, inconsistent attendance, or even overachievement driven by perfectionism. Students may not say, "I am overwhelmed," but they express it through silence, behavior, or resistance.

Teachers who protect the vulnerable pay attention to these signals. They ask thoughtful questions, offer flexibility, and create opportunities for students to share without fear. They understand that every behavior has a story behind it, and they seek to understand before making judgments.

Protective teachers also advocate. They speak up in individualized education plan meetings, collaborate with counselors, and ensure students receive the support they are entitled to. They push for inclusive practices and refuse to allow any student to become invisible.

Real Life Example: The Safe Chair

In a small elementary school in Nebraska, Mr. Ortiz created a space called the Safe Chair. It was not a place for punishment or time out. It was a designated area where students could go when they felt overwhelmed, frustrated, or sad. There were no questions and no judgment. It was simply a moment to pause, breathe, and signal the need for support.

Over time, the Safe Chair transformed the classroom environment. Students began using it not to avoid work, but to regulate their emotions. Mr. Ortiz protected his most vulnerable students not through discipline, but by providing space for recovery and return.

Protection Through Routines and Predictability

One of the most overlooked forms of protection is consistency. Many students come from environments that are unpredictable or chaotic. For them, a structured classroom is not restrictive. It is safe.

Knowing what to expect, following consistent routines, and trusting that the teacher will respond with fairness reduces anxiety and builds trust. Predictability allows students to focus on learning rather than survival.

Teachers who maintain structure and clear expectations create a protective environment. They are not rigid or authoritarian. They are steady. They enforce boundaries with empathy, creating a space where vulnerability is not punished, but respected.

Protection as Empowerment

Protecting the vulnerable does not mean viewing students as helpless. True protection empowers students. It helps them find their voice, understand their rights, and develop the ability to advocate for themselves and others.

This may include teaching conflict resolution, encouraging reflection, or supporting students as they speak up about challenges or injustice. It is reminding them that their feelings are valid and that their safety matters.

Protective teachers equip students with the tools they need long after they leave the classroom.

Additional Example: The ELL Advocate

Ms. Navarro teaches high school English in a district with a growing population of English language learners. One of her students, Ahmed, had recently immigrated and spoke very little English. Some teachers viewed him as disengaged.

Ms. Navarro saw something different. She paired him with a bilingual student and connected with his family to learn about his interests. She discovered that he loved storytelling. She began inviting him to share stories through images and recorded voice.

One day, Ahmed read a paragraph aloud in English for the first time. The class applauded. He smiled. He was no longer invisible.

Ms. Navarro protected his dignity while supporting his growth. She created space for success without forcing him into a narrow mold.

Digital Safety and Emotional Boundaries

In today's world, protection extends into digital spaces. Cyberbullying, harmful content, and the emotional effects of online interactions can significantly impact vulnerable students.

Teachers who prioritize digital literacy, establish respectful communication norms, and model healthy technology use protect students from these unseen risks.

At the same time, teachers must protect their own wellbeing. Supporting students does not mean absorbing every burden. Compassion fatigue is real. Knowing when to seek support from counselors, colleagues, or administrators is essential for sustainable leadership.

Responding, Not Reacting

When students act out, withdraw, or break rules, a protective teacher pauses before responding. Instead of reacting immediately, they ask, "What does this student need right now?" and "What is this behavior communicating?"

This approach does not eliminate boundaries. It strengthens them. Discipline and protection can exist together. Protective teachers hold students accountable while maintaining dignity.

A simple check in, a restorative conversation, or addressing behavior privately instead of publicly can build lasting trust.

Trauma Informed Practices

Educators around the world are increasingly using trauma informed approaches. These approaches recognize that many students carry unseen burdens and that behavior is often a symptom rather than the root issue.

Effective trauma informed strategies include:

Creating predictable routines

Offering choices to increase student ownership

Building strong relationships

Avoiding public embarrassment

Teaching emotional regulation skills

A trauma informed classroom does not lower expectations. It strengthens the foundation that allows students to meet them.

Reflective Takeaway

Protecting the vulnerable is not separate from teaching. It is teaching.

Every classroom includes students who need extra care, deeper patience, and a sense of belonging that extends beyond academics.

As a teacher, you are not expected to solve every problem. However, your consistent presence, your advocacy, and your willingness to adjust create protection that shapes lives.

Like the shepherd who watches closely and ensures no one is left behind, you hold space for those who might otherwise fall through the cracks.

And in doing so, you send a powerful message to every student, especially the most vulnerable ones, that they are worth the effort.

Because they are.

And so are you.

Reflection

Who in my classroom needs additional support right now?

How do I respond when a student displays behavior connected to trauma?

Are my classroom responses corrective or restorative?

Discussion Prompt

What does trauma informed practice look like in our school?

Research Anchor

Trauma informed approaches improve student regulation and academic outcomes (SAMHSA, 2014).

Chapter 4:
Guiding Through the Unknown

The Shepherd's Role

A shepherd's journey is rarely straight. Hills turn into valleys, trails disappear in storms, and visibility can change in an instant. The terrain does not come with a map, and danger can appear without warning, whether from predators, sudden weather, or shifting conditions. Yet, despite all of this, the flock continues to move forward.

They move forward not because they understand every turn, but because they trust the one leading them.

When the path ahead is unclear, the shepherd remains steady. The role is not to know every detail of what is coming, but to move with discernment, patience, and courage. The shepherd listens for danger, studies the land, and adjusts direction when necessary. Their strength is not found in certainty, but in commitment.

They do not panic when something goes wrong. They pause, reassess, and find another way. In doing so, they guide the flock with quiet confidence.

The Teacher's Role

Every school year brings uncertainty. New policies, new students, and new challenges require constant adjustment. Teachers enter classrooms with thoughtful plans, only to see those plans shift throughout the day or week.

Guiding through the unknown is not just a responsibility. It is a defining characteristic of effective teaching. You do not always know what lies ahead. It could be a sudden disruption, a community crisis, or an unexpected change in student behavior. Still, you continue to guide.

You lead when the curriculum changes midyear. You adjust when a lesson does not go as planned or when technology fails. You respond when a student needs something different than what you prepared.

This flexibility is not a weakness. It is wisdom in action. Just as a shepherd cannot control the weather, a teacher cannot control every classroom variable. What can be controlled is the response.

Building Resilience in Uncertain Times

One of the most powerful roles a teacher plays is modeling resilience. When the path is unclear, students watch how you respond. Do you react with frustration, or do you adapt with calm and purpose?

Perfection is not required. In fact, acknowledging that something is difficult and demonstrating how to keep moving forward is one of the most valuable lessons you can teach.

Saying, “I do not know how this will work yet, but we will figure it out together,” builds trust, strengthens community, and creates emotional safety.

Resilient teachers help develop resilient students. When students observe you adjusting calmly, they learn that uncertainty is not failure. It is an opportunity for growth.

Real Life Example: The Teacher Who Rebuilt Midyear

Ms. Langston was in her fifth year teaching fifth grade when her school suddenly transitioned to remote learning. At first, she tried to replicate her in person schedule online. It did not work. Attendance dropped, engagement declined, and she felt overwhelmed.

Instead of continuing with a model that was not effective, she asked students and families what they needed. She reduced screen time, created shorter recorded lessons, and scheduled weekly check ins by phone.

It was not perfect, but it was effective. Students reengaged. Families felt supported. When they returned to in person learning, they remembered how she guided them through uncertainty with purpose rather than panic.

Teaching Without All the Answers

Teachers are often expected to have all the answers. In reality, the most effective teachers are willing to admit when they do not know something and demonstrate how to find it.

This approach models lifelong learning and encourages curiosity. It also reduces the pressure of perfection for both teachers and students.

When a student asks a question you cannot answer, you might respond by saying:

"Let us research that together."

"That is a great question. I will look into it and follow up."

"I am not sure yet. Let us figure it out."

By guiding students through uncertainty rather than avoiding it, you show that learning is a process, not a final destination.

Embracing the Process

Uncertainty is not always the result of a crisis. It is often part of the learning experience.

A student writing a personal narrative for the first time may feel unsure. A group conducting a science experiment may feel frustrated when results do not match expectations. A class discussing complex topics may struggle to begin.

These moments are opportunities to guide students through the unknown, not by providing immediate answers, but by helping them ask meaningful questions.

Effective teachers facilitate discovery. They create space for struggle and provide support without removing the challenge.

Guiding students through uncertainty strengthens critical thinking, persistence, and creativity.

Additional Example: The Math Teacher Who Reframed Failure

Mr. Chen taught middle school mathematics. When students encountered challenging problems, they often said, "I do not understand," and stopped trying.

He shifted the classroom approach.

Instead of simply marking answers as incorrect, he added a section called "Stuck Point." Students identified where they became confused and explained what they had attempted.

This simple change transformed the classroom. Students no longer feared mistakes. They began to engage with the process.

Mr. Chen would say, "My role is not to make sure you never get stuck. My role is to help you learn how to move forward when you do."

This is guidance through uncertainty.

Practices for Navigating the Unknown

Teachers can use several strategies to guide effectively through uncertainty:

Stay grounded in values.

When situations feel uncertain, return to your purpose. Reflect on why you became a teacher and what you believe about learning and students. Let these beliefs guide your decisions.

Design flexible plans

Create lessons with multiple approaches so you can adjust when needed without hesitation.

Encourage student ownership

Involve students in creating expectations, projects, and classroom norms. When students have a role, they feel more confident navigating uncertainty.

Use regular checkpoints

Feedback tools, reflections, and discussions help you understand where students are academically and emotionally.

Normalize uncertainty

Acknowledge that confusion is a natural part of learning. Celebrate persistence as much as achievement.

The Power of Presence

At times, guiding through the unknown simply means being present. A steady and supportive presence can be more impactful than perfect instruction.

When students feel uncertain about school, their future, or themselves, they need someone who remains calm, consistent, and encouraging.

You do not need to have every answer. You need to remain committed.

In a constantly changing world, your presence becomes an anchor. Your belief in students becomes their direction. Your classroom becomes a starting point for discovery.

Reflective Takeaway

Teachers are not leaders because they have a perfect plan.

They are leaders because they are willing to move forward with courage, curiosity, and care, even when the path is unclear.

You are not expected to remove all uncertainty. You are called to walk through it alongside your students.

The path may not always be visible, but with your guidance, it remains possible.

Because you do more than teach content. You help shape futures.

And that is the essence of leadership in uncertain moments.

Reflection

How do I respond when I do not have the answers?

Do I normalize struggle for my students?

Where might I be modeling fear instead of adaptability?

Discussion Prompt

How can we intentionally build resilience into instruction?

Research Anchor

Research on growth mindset shows that framing struggle as part of learning increases perseverance and long-term success (Dweck, 2006).

Chapter 5: Creating Safe Pastures

The Shepherd's Role

A wise shepherd understands that safety is not only about keeping predators away. It is about creating an environment where the flock can rest, grow, and thrive. A good pasture is more than a patch of grass. It is a carefully selected, prepared, and maintained space. It is free from hidden dangers, with no sharp rocks, no thorn bushes, and no nearby threats. It provides fresh water, adequate shade, and room to move.

In a healthy pasture, sheep relax. They lie down. They graze without fear. This is where growth happens. When they feel secure, they shift from survival to flourishing.

The shepherd creates this space with intention. They do not assume the pasture is safe. They inspect it. They remove risks. They remain present.

For the shepherd, safety is not an afterthought. It is the foundation for everything else.

The Teacher's Role

For teachers, the classroom is the pasture. It must be a space where students feel safe, not only physically, but also emotionally, socially, and intellectually.

In unsafe classrooms, students withdraw. They hesitate to ask questions, avoid taking risks, and hold back their ideas. Instead of focusing on learning, they focus on protecting themselves. They wonder if they will be embarrassed, judged, or excluded.

Safe classrooms allow students to show up fully. They bring their questions, creativity, insecurities, and aspirations. In these environments, learning can truly take root.

Psychological Safety in Action

Psychological safety is the belief that students can speak, take risks, and make mistakes without fear of embarrassment or punishment. It does not mean a lack of structure or expectations. It means that effort and risk taking are encouraged, and mistakes are viewed as part of growth.

Practices that build psychological safety include:

Valuing student voice consistently

Responding to incorrect answers with curiosity rather than criticism

Reinforcing that effort is more important than perfection

Creating routines that normalize vulnerability, such as sharing a meaningful mistake and what was learned

Students grow when they feel safe enough to try, fail, and try again.

Real Life Example: A Culture of Celebration

At a middle school in Oregon, Ms. Pike introduced a weekly tradition called Risk Taker Friday. Throughout the week, she recorded the names of students who demonstrated courage by participating, trying something new, or sharing honestly.

Each Friday, she recognized those students and celebrated their effort rather than their accuracy.

The impact was immediate. Students stopped fearing mistakes and began engaging more deeply. Participation increased, and students who had once been quiet began contributing to discussions.

The classroom became a space where learning felt safe, open, and supportive.

Building Emotional Safety

Students bring their emotions with them into the classroom. They carry experiences from home, stress from their environment, and insecurities shaped over time.

Emotionally safe classrooms recognize this reality. Teachers who create emotional safety:

Greet students warmly and by name

Pay attention to changes in mood or behavior

Acknowledge emotions without judgment

Teach strategies for self-regulation such as breathing, movement, or journaling

This is not about replacing professional support services. It is about being a caring adult who recognizes and responds to the whole student.

Social Safety and Belonging

Every student enters the classroom with a fundamental question: Do I belong here?

Classrooms that affirm identity, respect differences, and promote inclusion answer that question with confidence. Social safety means students do not fear judgment from their peers. It means that exclusion is addressed, kindness is expected, and respect is modeled.

Representation also matters. When students see their cultures, languages, families, and experiences reflected in the classroom, they feel more secure in being themselves.

Teachers foster social safety by:

Structuring groups to encourage inclusion

Modeling respectful communication

Establishing clear expectations for language and behavior

Incorporating diverse materials and perspectives

Additional Example: The Circle Time Shift

In a second grade classroom in Detroit, Ms. Walters noticed tension during transitions. Students argued frequently, and some were consistently excluded.

She introduced daily ten-minute community circles. Each student responded to a simple prompt such as, "What is something you are proud of today?" or "What is one kind thing someone did for you?"

At first, responses were brief. Over time, students became more open. Relationships strengthened. Conflicts decreased. Empathy grew.

The classroom environment changed, not through control, but through intentional connection

Intellectual Safety and Risk Taking

Learning requires risk. Students must be willing to say, "I do not understand yet." This level of honesty requires a safe environment.

Teachers build intellectual safety by:

Valuing questions as much as answers

Encouraging multiple strategies for solving problems

Using mistakes as opportunities for learning

Recognizing effort and progress rather than only outcomes

When students are not penalized for uncertainty, they begin to engage more deeply with learning.

Classroom Management as Safety

Classroom management is often viewed as controlling behavior. It can be reframed as creating a sense of safety.

Clear expectations, consistent routines, and fair consequences help students feel secure. When students understand what to expect and trust that they will be treated fairly, they are more likely to engage.

Effective classroom management is built on clarity and consistency. It is not about control. It is about trust.

Creating Safe Environments in Uncertain Times

During times of community stress, uncertainty, or crisis, classrooms can become places of stability. Teachers who maintain calm, allow space for conversation, and provide reassurance help students navigate difficult moments.

Sometimes safety is created through consistency:

The routine continues

The structure remains

The teacher is present and steady

In uncertain times, the classroom becomes a place where students can find calm and focus.

The Hidden Power of Safety

When students feel safe, their ability to learn increases. Research in educational neuroscience shows that students in supportive environments retain information more effectively, take academic risks, and demonstrate greater motivation.

Safety is not an added benefit in education. It is essential.

Reflective Takeaway

Creating safe environments is not a onetime action. It is a daily commitment. It is reflected in how you greet students, how you respond to mistakes, how you set expectations, and how you listen.

The safety you create may not always be visible, but its impact can be seen in participation, confidence, and trust.

You are not just managing a classroom. You are shaping an environment where students can grow.

And in that environment, they do more than learn. They develop.

Because they feel safe.

Because you created that space.

Reflection

Would my students describe this classroom as emotionally safe?

How do I respond to incorrect answers?

What routines help create consistency and predictability?

Discussion Prompt

What does psychological safety look like in our school community?

Research Anchor

Psychological safety increases engagement, risk taking, and learning outcomes (Edmondson, 2018).

Part II: The Work of the Shepherd

Chapter 6:
Feeding the Hungry

The Shepherd's Role

For a shepherd, feeding the flock is more than a task. It is an act of care, sustenance, and preparation for the journey ahead. Sheep need more than any patch of grass. They require nourishment that matches their stage of development, the season they are in, and the terrain they are crossing. A shepherd understands that too little food weakens the body, while poor quality nourishment leads to long term harm. True nourishment requires attentiveness.

Some sheep require additional care, including those recovering from illness, newly weaned lambs, or ewes preparing to give birth. The shepherd ensures that each member of the flock receives what it needs at the right time.

Feeding is not only about physical sustenance. It builds trust. Sheep associate their shepherd with provision, with the place where their needs are met and their wellbeing is sustained.

The Teacher's Role

In the classroom, feeding the hungry means nourishing the mind, the heart, and sometimes even the body. Students arrive each day with a wide range of academic, emotional, and physical needs. Some are intellectually under challenged and are seeking deeper meaning and purpose. Others are emotionally exhausted and need encouragement, connection, and reassurance.

Effective teachers recognize these needs and respond with intention. They challenge students while remaining supportive. They offer structure while maintaining compassion. Their instruction is not only aligned to standards, but also to the real human needs in front of them.

Academic Nourishment

Academic hunger presents itself in different ways. Some students are eager to learn and want more than what is presented. Others disengage because the content does not feel relevant or meaningful.

Teachers provide academic nourishment by:

Offering rich, relevant, and rigorous content

Adjusting instruction to meet students at their current level

Incorporating student voice and choice into learning

Connecting lessons to real world experiences and student interests

A nourished mind becomes curious, and curiosity leads to lifelong learning.

Real Life Example: The Debate Club Catalyst

At an urban high school in New York, Ms. Rivera noticed a group of students who rarely spoke during class but engaged in passionate discussions in the cafeteria. Rather than viewing this as a distraction, she recognized potential.

She created an informal lunch debate group and introduced topics connected to current events and classroom content. Over time, those same students began participating in class, producing stronger work, and mentoring others.

Ms. Rivera did more than meet academic needs. She affirmed student voice and potential.

Emotional Nourishment

Students also need emotional support. They seek belonging, encouragement, and hope. Emotional nourishment may look like:

Noticing when a student is quieter than usual

Offering encouragement after a challenging moment

Recognizing effort as well as achievement

Allowing space for joy, reflection, or even frustration

Teachers who provide emotional support help students build confidence and a sense of belonging. Students begin to believe that they matter.

The Power of Feedback

Nourishment is not found in empty praise. It comes from feedback that is specific, meaningful, and focused on growth.

Instead of general praise, teachers can say:

"I noticed how you improved your explanation. That shows strong thinking."

"You stayed focused even when it was challenging. That persistence matters."

This type of feedback builds independence and encourages continuous growth rather than dependence on approval.

Additional Example: Notes That Feed

Mr. Daniels, a high school history teacher, developed a simple routine. Each Friday, he wrote a short note of encouragement for every student. Each note was personal and specific.

Examples included:

"Your question helped others understand the topic better."

"I saw your focus this week. Keep it going."

"You are someone others can rely on."

Students began saving these notes. Some kept them in their notebooks.

Others displayed them as reminders.

One student shared that it was the first time a teacher had told them they were good at something.

Mr. Daniels nourished not only learning, but also identity.

Physical Nourishment and Equity

Sometimes feeding the hungry includes meeting physical needs. Many teachers keep snacks available, provide quiet support to students in need, or connect families with resources.

They understand that a student who is physically hungry cannot fully engage in learning.

Teachers also advocate for programs such as school meals, food support initiatives, and community partnerships. These efforts promote dignity and ensure that basic needs are met.

Nourishing Through Connection

Connection is essential for learning. Teachers nourish students by being present and intentional in their interactions. This includes:

Making eye contact

Using student names

Listening attentively

Sharing appropriate personal experiences

When students feel connected, they are more willing to engage, participate, and take ownership of their learning.

Culturally Responsive Teaching as Nourishment

A single approach to teaching does not meet the needs of all students. Culturally responsive teaching ensures that instruction reflects students' identities, experiences, and communities.

This may include:

Incorporating diverse authors and perspectives

Using examples that reflect student experiences

Inviting students to share their cultural knowledge

When students see themselves in their learning, they feel valued and more engaged.

Supporting Advanced Learners

Some students require greater challenge to stay engaged. Without appropriate support, they may become disengaged or lose motivation.

Teachers can support advanced learners by:

Offering independent or extended learning opportunities

Providing choices in assignments

Connecting students with mentors or additional resources

Encouraging them to support peers

Every student deserves to be challenged and supported.

The Burnout Challenge: Supporting the Teacher

Teachers give continuously to their students. Without support, this can lead to exhaustion.

Just as students need nourishment, teachers do as well. This includes:

Setting healthy boundaries

Recognizing personal progress

Building connections with colleagues

Engaging in learning that inspires growth

Supporting others requires maintaining your own wellbeing.

Reflective Takeaway

Teaching is an act of nourishment.

When you support a student intellectually, emotionally, or physically, you do more than deliver instruction. You demonstrate care, belief, and commitment.

You do not have to meet every need. But each day, you offer something meaningful. A word, a lesson, or a moment of encouragement.

These small actions have lasting impact.

You nourish confidence.
You strengthen identity.
You shape futures.

One moment at a time.

Reflection

Which students need greater challenge?

Which students need additional support?

How can I maintain high expectations while meeting diverse needs?

Discussion Prompt

How does our curriculum address and support diverse learning needs?

Research Anchor

Differentiated instruction improves engagement and academic outcomes when aligned with student readiness levels (Tomlinson, 2014).

Chapter 7: Finding the Lost

The Shepherd's Role

In every flock, sheep sometimes wander. They lose sight of the group, become distracted, or simply lose their direction. Some drift far away, while others move just enough to be at risk. A shepherd does not ignore these moments or abandon the sheep. They notice, and they go after them.

Finding the lost is one of the clearest expressions of a shepherd's care. It requires time, effort, and sometimes risk. It may involve climbing difficult terrain, navigating obstacles, or traveling long distances to bring one sheep back.

To the shepherd, each one matters.

This act of leaving the many to find the one is not about numbers. It is about value. Every sheep is known, counted, and worth bringing back.

The Teacher's Role

In the classroom, students become lost for many reasons. Some withdraw quietly, overwhelmed by academic demands or social pressures. Others push away through defiance or disengagement. Some go unnoticed for long periods of time, with their potential overlooked and their voices unheard.

Effective teachers notice these changes. They pay attention to shifts in behavior, sudden quietness, or subtle signs of withdrawal. They do not dismiss students who struggle or disconnect. Instead, they respond with care, creativity, and persistence.

They do not ask, "What is wrong with you?" They ask, "What has happened, and how can I support you?"

The Many Faces of Being Lost

Being lost can take many forms:

A student who stops completing assignments

A student who once engaged but now avoids eye contact

A high performing student whose performance suddenly declines

A social student who becomes withdrawn

A new student who struggles to adjust

Being lost is not only academic. It is emotional, mental, and relational.

Students often do not ask for help directly. This is why teachers must remain observant and responsive.

Real Life Example: The Headphones Student

In a suburban middle school, Ms. Barnes had a student named Jada who wore large headphones every day. She rarely spoke, and some teachers viewed her behavior as defiant.

Ms. Barnes approached her with curiosity and asked, "Does the music help you focus?"

Jada hesitated, then said quietly, "It blocks everything out."

Instead of removing the headphones, Ms. Barnes offered a compromise. She suggested using one earbud during work time and invited Jada to talk after class.

Over time, conversations revealed that Jada's home environment was overwhelming. The headphones were not defiance. They were a way to cope.

Gradually, the headphones came off, and Jada began to reengage.

One student was found.

Looking Beyond the Surface

To find the lost, teachers must look beyond visible behaviors and academic performance. A smile does not always indicate that everything is fine. A quiet student is not always content. A loud student is not always confident.

Finding the lost requires listening without judgment, asking thoughtful questions, and creating opportunities for students to be seen and heard.

Some helpful practices include:

Simple check in forms that ask students how they are feeling

Anonymous spaces where students can share concerns

Small group conversations that encourage openness

Relationships First

Academic progress often begins with connection. When students feel known and valued, they are more likely to engage and participate.

Building relationships does not require large amounts of time. It can be done through small, meaningful actions:

Remembering important details about a student's life

Asking about their experiences outside of school

Following up on previous conversations

Noticing changes in behavior or mood

Finding the lost is about making it clear that every student matters and is seen.

Additional Example: The Reading Breakthrough

Mr. Scott taught third grade. One of his students, Tyler, struggled with reading and was performing below grade level. Tyler often disrupted class and had difficulty staying engaged.

Instead of focusing only on discipline, Mr. Scott gave Tyler a role as a reading helper. Tyler organized books, read aloud in a low pressure setting, and helped select materials for the class.

Over time, Tyler's reading skills improved, and his behavior changed. He became more engaged and confident.

Tyler did not need punishment. He needed purpose and encouragement.

Partnering with Families

Finding the lost often involves connecting with families. Caregivers may not be aware of what is happening at school or may be facing their own challenges.

Approaching families with understanding rather than judgment helps build trust:

"I have noticed that Jamal seems more tired lately. I wanted to check in and see how we can support him."

"Ava has been quieter than usual. I would love to work together to support her."

When families feel supported, they are more likely to engage in the process.

Finding the Lost in Groups

Sometimes entire groups of students are overlooked. These may include students who sit quietly, students in lower level courses, or those facing language or learning challenges.

Teachers who prioritize equity ask important questions:

Who is not participating?

Who is not present consistently?

Who is not showing progress, and why?

They respond by adjusting instruction, increasing accessibility, and creating opportunities for all students to engage.

Often, the students who are most in need of support are the least visible.

Finding Without Fixing

Finding the lost does not mean solving every problem. It means showing up consistently.

Sometimes, support looks like:
Sitting beside a student in silence
Walking with a student to access additional support
Offering reassurance and presence
These actions communicate a powerful message. The student is not alone.

You may not always have answers, but your willingness to show up can make a lasting difference.

When the Teacher Feels Lost

Teachers may also experience moments of feeling overwhelmed or uncertain. In these times, it is important to remember:

You are not alone
Seeking support is a sign of strength
You deserve care and encouragement as well
Colleagues, mentors, and support staff can provide guidance and reassurance when needed.

Even those who guide others need support.

Reflective Takeaway

Finding the lost is meaningful and important work.

You may not always know who needs support the most, but your attention, persistence, and care can create powerful change.

Students who were once disengaged may later recognize your impact. They may remember that you were the one who noticed and cared.

Being found is not only about location. It is about dignity and belonging.

Every student deserves that.

You are the one who notices.
You are the one who reaches out.
You are the one who brings them back.

Keep going.

Reflection

Which students have quietly disengaged?

How quickly do I respond when I notice changes?

What signals indicate that a student may be struggling?

Discussion Prompt

What systems do we have in place for early support and intervention?

Research Anchor

Strong relationships between teachers and students are associated with increased engagement and reduced risk of dropout (Rumberger, 2011).

Chapter 8: Listening for the Cry

The Shepherd's Role

A seasoned shepherd does more than watch over the flock. They listen. In the quiet of the field, a shepherd learns to distinguish between ordinary sounds and signals of distress. One sound may indicate hunger. Another may signal fear. A different cry may reveal that a lamb is stuck or separated from the group.

The shepherd becomes attentive.

They do not wait for a crisis to unfold. At the first sign of struggle, they respond. Listening becomes a way to prevent harm, not just react to it. The shepherd understands that each sound carries meaning. It is not noise. It is communication.

The Teacher's Role

Students communicate in many ways, and not all of them involve words. Their expressions of need may appear as silence, humor, body language, or sudden changes in behavior. Effective teachers learn to understand these signals. They do not simply hear. They listen with intention.

Listening for the cry means recognizing what students are trying to express beneath their actions. A slammed book may reflect frustration or self doubt. A sarcastic remark may hide fear. A student who falls asleep in class may be dealing with challenges outside of school.

When teachers listen deeply, students feel understood. Feeling understood is often the first step toward growth and healing.

Creating a Culture of Listening

Listening is an active practice. It requires focus, patience, and a willingness to pause.

Teachers who create a culture of listening:

Pause and give attention when students speak

Ask thoughtful follow up questions

Reflect understanding by restating what they hear

Acknowledge and validate student emotions

This approach helps students understand that their voices matter, even when they struggle to express themselves clearly.

Real Life Example: The Writing Assignment

In a tenth grade English class in Georgia, Ms. Li assigned a personal narrative. A quiet student named Anthony submitted a story about witnessing his older brother being arrested.

Rather than focusing only on writing mechanics, Ms. Li responded with care. She wrote, "Thank you for sharing your story. It took courage to express this."

The following day, Anthony stayed after class to talk. That moment led to deeper engagement, stronger writing, and eventually a college essay based on his experience.

Ms. Li recognized more than an assignment. She recognized a student's voice.

Looking Beyond Behavior

Behavior is a form of communication. Students rarely act out without a reason. Their actions often reflect deeper emotions or unmet needs.

A student who uses humor constantly may be protecting themselves from insecurity. A student who gives up quickly may fear failure. A student who challenges authority may be seeking a sense of control.

Listening asks a deeper question. What is this student trying to communicate?

When teachers listen without judgment, they build trust and understanding.

Listening with Awareness

Students communicate through many signals:

Body language such as posture and movement

Tone of voice and shifts in expression

Patterns in work completion and effort

Teachers who observe these patterns and ask thoughtful questions create opportunities for meaningful conversations.

For example:

"I noticed you have seemed quieter this week. How are you doing?"

"You looked frustrated earlier. Would you like to talk about it?"

Students are more likely to respond when they feel seen and respected.

Additional Example: The Listening Space

At an elementary school in Wisconsin, Mr. Ray created a designated space where students could sit when they wanted to talk. It was not used for discipline. It was simply a place for conversation.

When a student sat there, Mr. Ray gave his full attention. No distractions. No interruptions.

Over time, students began to open up. Some shared concerns. Others shared experiences or feelings they had been holding inside.

One student expressed that it was the only place where they felt truly heard.

Listening does not require a special space. It requires presence, time, and care.

Listening in a Busy World

Students today experience constant stimulation from technology, social interactions, and external pressures. They often carry more than they realize.

Teachers can provide a moment of calm and focus. A simple question, a brief check in, or a quiet moment of attention can make a significant difference.

When students realize that someone is genuinely listening, they begin to open up.

When Students Speak for Others

At times, students share concerns about their peers. They may express worry about bullying, behavior, or safety.

These moments require thoughtful response. Teachers should:

Take concerns seriously

Follow appropriate procedures for support

Thank students for sharing their concerns

Responding with care ensures that students feel safe coming forward and that important issues are addressed.

Listening Through Student Work

Students often reveal their thoughts and emotions through assignments, creative work, and written expression. A story, drawing, or journal entry can provide insight into their experiences.

Teachers who respond with curiosity rather than judgment create opportunities for connection.

A simple response such as, "Your writing expresses something meaningful. Would you like to share more about it?" can open the door to important conversations.

Maintaining Boundaries

Listening does not mean carrying every burden alone. Teachers play an important role, but they are not expected to manage every situation independently.

When students share serious concerns:

Acknowledge their courage

Be clear about your role

Connect them with appropriate support resources

Reassuring students that they are not alone helps them feel supported while ensuring they receive the help they need.

Reflective Takeaway

Listening for the cry is both a skill and a responsibility. It transforms the classroom into a place where students feel safe to express themselves.

Every student has a voice, even when it is hidden.

As a teacher, you have the opportunity to notice, to listen, and to respond with care.

You do not need perfect words. You need awareness and compassion.

When students feel heard, they begin to grow. When they grow, they begin to believe in themselves again.

You are the one who listens.

You are the one who notices.
You are the one who responds.

Continue listening. Your presence matters.

Reflection

Do I listen with the intent to understand or to respond?

How often do I create space for emotional check ins?

Which student behaviors may reflect deeper needs?

Discussion Prompt

How can we strengthen a culture of listening throughout our school?

Research Anchor

Research shows that emotional awareness in educators contributes to stronger classroom environments and improved student outcomes (Brackett et al., 2011).

Chapter 9:
Protecting the Flock

The Shepherd's Role

A shepherd's protection is not passive. It is proactive. It requires constant awareness, recognizing danger before it becomes visible, and placing oneself between the flock and harm. Whether the threat comes from predators, harsh weather, or unsafe terrain, the shepherd takes action before the flock is affected.

Protection also requires presence. When sheep sense that the shepherd is near, they rest. They explore. They move with confidence because they trust that someone is watching over them.

This trust is not built in a single moment. It is developed through consistent actions over time. Staying close, guiding with clarity, and responding with courage create a sense of security that allows the flock to thrive.

The Teacher's Role

Teachers protect students in many ways. They protect them from academic failure, emotional harm, social exclusion, and systems that may overlook or disadvantage them. The classroom becomes more than a place of instruction. It becomes a protected space where students can grow, question, and develop.

Protection in the classroom is not always obvious. It may appear as a quiet redirection, a consistent expectation, or a firm boundary delivered with care. At other times, it requires standing up clearly and confidently when a student is treated unfairly or overlooked.

Teachers are not only educators. They are advocates and protectors.

Physical and Emotional Safety

Protection begins with creating an environment that is physically and emotionally secure.

Physically safe classrooms:

Maintain clear procedures for emergencies

Provide organized and accessible spaces

Ensure all students are supervised and accounted for

Emotionally safe classrooms:

Address bullying and harmful language immediately

Promote respect and inclusion

Establish consistent expectations for behavior

When students feel safe, they are better able to focus, engage, and learn. Safety supports structure, and structure supports growth.

Real Life Example: The Advocate

Ms. Gonzales, a high school science teacher in Texas, noticed that a student named Kai was repeatedly misidentified by peers. Many adults were unsure how to respond.

Ms. Gonzales chose to act. She met with Kai, listened carefully, and implemented changes. She provided guidance to staff on respectful language, created visible signs of support in her classroom, and reinforced expectations for respectful interactions.

Kai later wrote, "You were the first adult who addressed what was happening. You made me feel safe."

Protecting students means recognizing harm and addressing it directly.

Protecting from Overwhelm

Protection also includes managing the pace of learning. Teachers support students by ensuring that expectations are challenging but achievable.

This may involve:

Breaking tasks into manageable steps

Incorporating moments of creativity and engagement

Providing opportunities to revisit and improve work

Effective learning environments challenge students while also supporting their wellbeing. Growth does not require unnecessary stress.

Teachers also model balance. When teachers demonstrate healthy habits, students learn to value their own wellbeing.

Systems Level Protection

Some challenges extend beyond the classroom. These may include limited access to resources, bias within systems, or gaps in student support.

Teachers act as protectors when they:

Advocate during meetings and discussions

Collaborate with support staff

Communicate with leadership

Work toward improving systems that impact students

Protection at this level often requires persistence and commitment.

Additional Example: The Policy Change

At a middle school, Mr. Brooks noticed that several students were frequently late due to unreliable transportation. These students were being penalized despite circumstances beyond their control.

He gathered information, presented his findings, and worked with school leadership to adjust arrival policies. As a result, students experienced less stress and improved engagement.

One student shared that they no longer felt discouraged upon arriving at school.

Mr. Brooks demonstrated that protection can extend beyond the classroom.

Protecting Identity and Dignity

Students bring their identities, cultures, and experiences into the classroom. Protection includes honoring and respecting these aspects of who they are.

Teachers protect student dignity by:

Using correct names and pronunciations

Including diverse perspectives in learning materials

Challenging stereotypes and bias

Encouraging students to share their experiences

When students feel respected, they are more confident and engaged.

Protecting Peer Relationships

Teachers influence the way students interact with one another. They establish expectations for communication and behavior.

This includes:

Modeling respectful dialogue

Teaching social and emotional skills

Supporting students in resolving conflicts

Encouraging accountability and understanding

Healthy relationships contribute to a positive and supportive learning environment.

Taking Action

There are moments when teachers must act immediately to protect students. This may involve:

Addressing inappropriate comments or behavior

Intervening in conflicts

Reporting concerns to appropriate personnel

Students remember when someone stands up for them. Protection requires courage and consistency.

When Teachers Need Support

Teachers also need safe environments. Supporting students should not come at the expense of personal wellbeing.

Teachers can protect themselves by:

Seeking support from colleagues and leadership

Setting appropriate boundaries

Utilizing available resources

Collaboration strengthens the ability to support students effectively.

Reflective Takeaway

Protection is an expression of care and commitment.

It is not about restriction. It is about creating conditions where students can feel confident and capable.

When students trust that their dignity will be respected, they are more willing to take risks, share ideas, and engage in learning.

You provide stability, advocacy, and support.

Your actions influence how students view themselves and their environment.

Protection is not only something you do. It is part of who you are as an educator.

You create a space where students can learn, grow, and feel secure.

Because of you, they are safe.

Reflection

Do my students trust that I will support and protect them?

How do I respond when I notice subtle exclusion or bias?

Discussion Prompt

What does equitable support look like in daily practice?

Research Anchor

Research shows that culturally responsive teaching supports student engagement and academic success (Ladson Billings, 1995).

Chapter 10:
Restoring the Wounded

The Shepherd's Role

In the natural world, wounds are inevitable. A sheep may stumble on rough terrain, be scratched by brush, or encounter danger. When this happens, the shepherd does not turn away. They move toward the pain.

A shepherd cares for the injured with both tenderness and urgency. They clean the wound, apply healing balm, and make sure the injured sheep is not left behind. At times, the shepherd carries the wounded on their shoulders, slowing their pace to allow healing to take place.

Wounds are not treated as weaknesses. They are opportunities for care. They are moments when trust deepens and the shepherd's role becomes visible not only in guidance, but in restoration.

The Teacher's Role

Students often arrive carrying unseen wounds. Some are navigating recent trauma such as loss, instability, or hardship. Others carry deeper, long term challenges including self-doubt, inequity, or emotional struggles. Some experience pain within the classroom through peer interactions, academic setbacks, or personal frustration.

The teacher becomes a restorer. Not a fixer and not a therapist, but a steady presence that communicates, "You do not have to carry this alone."

Restoration means meeting students where they are. It means offering understanding before judgment, connection before correction, and care before consequence.

The Power of Gentle Response

A restorative teacher responds to student pain with empathy and patience. They do not rush the process or dismiss what a student is experiencing.

They:

Acknowledge the difficulty of the situation

Avoid minimizing language

Provide opportunities for students to express themselves

Reinforce that it is acceptable to struggle

Gentleness does not lower expectations. It strengthens relationships.

Real Life Example: The Locker Moment

Ms. Jackson, a middle school mathematics teacher, once noticed a student crying near their locker after school. She sat beside him and gently asked, "Would you like to talk, or would you prefer to sit quietly together?"

After several minutes, the student shared, "Everyone thinks I am not capable. Even at home."

Ms. Jackson did not rush to solve the problem. She simply said, "I do not see you that way, and I will show you that through how we work together."

That moment changed everything. The student began to engage more, complete assignments, and slowly rebuild confidence.

Recognizing Hidden Wounds

Many student challenges are not immediately visible. These may include:

Anxiety hidden behind humor

Fear masked by perfectionism

Quiet sadness concealed by compliance

Restoration requires time, trust, and consistency. Teachers support this process by:

Allowing opportunities to try again without shame

Following up after emotional moments

Providing meaningful responsibilities

Encouraging peer support and mentorship

Students often grow when someone believes in them before they believe in themselves.

Creating a Healing Environment

A restorative classroom provides space for students to feel supported and valued. It is an environment where students can be themselves while continuing to grow.

This includes:

Clear expectations combined with encouragement

Visible messages of affirmation

Spaces for reflection and emotional regulation

Consistent routines that provide stability

Structure, when paired with care, becomes supportive rather than restrictive.

The Role of Story and Identity

Stories are powerful tools for healing. When students share their experiences and hear the experiences of others, they begin to feel less alone.

Teachers support restoration by:

Encouraging personal expression through assignments

Using materials that reflect diverse experiences

Sharing appropriate personal examples of growth

Stories remind students that their experiences matter.

Additional Example: Creative Expression

In a high school art class, Mr. Norman noticed a student, Lila, creating artwork that reflected isolation and struggle.

Instead of redirecting her, he encouraged her to explore a theme of healing. Her final piece showed light emerging through broken glass.

Later, she shared that the class was one of the few places where she felt understood.

Creative expression can be a powerful path toward restoration.

Restoration Through Boundaries

Restoration includes both care and structure. Students feel supported when expectations are clear and consistent.

This includes:

Applying expectations fairly

Providing constructive responses

Addressing issues privately rather than publicly

Restorative teachers do not ignore challenges. They respond in ways that support growth and maintain dignity.

Collaboration and Support

Teachers are not expected to do this work alone. Counselors, support staff, and administrators are important partners in supporting students.

Teachers can:

Refer students to appropriate resources

Collaborate with support teams

Follow through on support plans

Working together strengthens outcomes for students and supports teachers as well.

When Teachers Need Restoration

Teachers also experience challenges. The responsibility of supporting others can be demanding.

Teachers benefit from:

Seeking support when needed

Developing personal routines for reflection and recovery

Connecting with supportive colleagues

Recognizing the impact of their work

Supporting others requires maintaining your own wellbeing.

Reflective Takeaway

Restoration is meaningful work that often goes unseen.

You are the one who slows down when needed. You are the presence that reassures and the voice that encourages.

You remind students:

That setbacks are not permanent

That challenges can be overcome

That they are more than their difficult moments

Because of you, students begin to rebuild confidence and hope.

Continue this work. It matters deeply.

Reflection

How do I respond when students struggle or fail?

Do I provide opportunities for growth and recovery?

How do I model resilience and healing?

Research Anchor

Restorative practices support improved behavior and a more positive school environment (González, 2015).

Part III: The Heart of the Teacher

Chapter 11: Watching Through the Night

The Shepherd's Role

When darkness settles over the land, the flock rests. The shepherd, however, remains alert. Even in stillness, they listen for signs of danger and stay ready to respond.

Night represents uncertainty and vulnerability. The shepherd's watchfulness provides protection even when it is not visible. The flock may not always see the shepherd, but they trust that care is present.

In these quiet moments, presence is the shepherd's greatest strength.

The Teacher's Role

Teachers carry a similar responsibility. Even after the school day ends, their thoughts often remain with their students. They reflect, plan, and consider how to support each learner.

This extended care is not limited to time. It reflects a mindset of dedication and responsibility.

Teachers prepare, anticipate, and continue to support students even when they are not physically present.

The Invisible Work

Much of teaching happens beyond the classroom. This includes:

Preparing lessons that engage students

Communicating with families

Exploring strategies to support individual needs

Reflecting on daily interactions

This work is often unseen, but it contributes significantly to student success.

Real Life Example: The Late Night Insight

Ms. Thompson, an elementary teacher, worked with a student named Elijah who struggled to remain focused. One evening, she researched strategies to better support him.

The next day, she introduced simple adjustments such as movement breaks and a focus tool.

These changes made an immediate difference. Elijah became more engaged, and his confidence improved.

His family later expressed gratitude for her continued effort and care.

The Responsibility of Care

Teachers carry more than instructional responsibilities. They also hold:

Awareness of student needs

Concern for student well being

A commitment to equity and opportunity

A desire to make a meaningful difference

This responsibility can be demanding, which is why balance is important.

Recognizing Signs Early

Teachers often notice changes before others do. These may include:

Shifts in behavior or mood

Changes in participation

Declines in academic performance

Responding early may involve:

Checking in with the student

Connecting with support staff

Communicating with families

Early awareness can prevent larger challenges.

Building Support Systems

Sustained care requires systems. Teachers can create structures such as:

Regular student checks ins

Tracking progress and patterns

Peer support systems

Encouraging student self-advocacy

Support systems help ensure that students are consistently supported.

Additional Example: The Observant Teacher

Mr. Lopez, a high school teacher, tracked patterns in student behavior and engagement. He noticed that one student had become withdrawn and less engaged.

After reaching out, he learned that the student was experiencing a difficult family situation. He worked with school staff to provide support.

The student later expressed appreciation for being noticed and supported during a challenging time.

Preparation and Care

Teachers prepare for both expected and unexpected situations. This includes:

Planning for transitions

Creating inclusive lessons

Preparing for potential challenges

Preparation reflects care and commitment to student success.

The Importance of Rest

Even the most dedicated teachers need rest. Sustained care requires balance.

Teachers can support themselves by:

Setting boundaries

Taking time to recharge

Engaging in personal interests

Building supportive relationships

Rest allows teachers to continue their work with clarity and energy.

Reflective Takeaway

Watching through the night represents a commitment that extends beyond visible moments.

You plan, reflect, and care deeply for your students. Your efforts, even when unseen, have lasting impact.

You provide stability, preparation, and support.

Continue your work with intention, but also allow yourself time to rest.

Your presence matters, both to your students and to yourself.

Reflection:

How do I manage the invisible labor of teaching?

What boundaries protect my sustainability?

Research Anchor:

Teacher burnout is significantly reduced by emotional boundary-setting and peer support (Maslach & Leiter, 2016).

Chapter 12: Leading Without Being Seen

The Shepherd's Role

A shepherd's influence is often most powerful when it is least visible. While the flock grazes, plays, or rests, the shepherd remains nearby, watching, guiding, and preparing, but rarely drawing attention to themselves. The sheep may not always be aware of the shepherd's presence, yet it is that very presence that keeps them safe and secure.

The shepherd does not demand recognition. Their leadership is quiet, persistent, and purposeful. They adjust direction without fanfare, guide wandering sheep without harshness, and step in only when necessary. The flock moves forward, often unaware that each safe step is possible because someone has been watching over them.

This is leadership through service. It is influence without applause.

The Teacher's Role

Teachers also lead without being seen. Much of what they do goes unnoticed, including weekend planning, after school calls to families, quiet check ins with students, and the extra time spent understanding a learning challenge or family hardship.

Students often do not realize the depth of effort their teachers invest until years later. Even then, the teacher's goal was never recognition. It was care.

Leading without being seen means choosing impact over image. It is the strength of humility and the wisdom of service.

Quiet Leadership in the Classroom

The most effective classroom leaders do not lead through control. They lead through presence. They:

Build routines that help students take ownership

Design learning environments that do not revolve around the teacher

Step back so students can step forward

These teachers trust students to lead discussions, manage responsibilities, and solve problems. When students succeed, the teacher quietly celebrates, knowing their influence helped shape the moment.

This type of leadership builds confidence rather than dependence.

Real Life Example: The Invisible Supporter

In a middle school in Michigan, Mr. Beale had a student named Rosa who struggled with anxiety. She dreaded speaking in front of the class.

Instead of forcing her to present or excusing her entirely, he offered options. She could record her presentation at home or present to him privately during lunch.

Over time, Rosa gained confidence. Eventually, she chose to present live in front of her classmates.

Years later, she returned and said, "You never made my struggle the center of attention. You quietly gave me room to grow, and that changed everything."

Mr. Beale helped her move beyond fear, not by putting her in the spotlight, but by creating space.

Leading in Staff Culture

Teachers also lead quietly in the way they treat colleagues. They lead by:

Encouraging a coworker who feels discouraged

Covering a responsibility without expecting recognition

Sharing resources and ideas freely

These actions create ripples. They influence school culture. Leadership is not about title. It is about impact.

Some of the strongest teacher leaders are not the loudest people in the room. They are the ones whose influence runs deepest.

The Hidden Curriculum

Teachers are always teaching, even when they are not delivering a formal lesson. Students learn from how teachers:

Respond to frustration

Treat challenging students

Handle failure and success

This is the hidden curriculum, the lessons taught by example.

When a teacher apologizes, students learn humility. When a teacher celebrates another person's idea, students learn generosity. When a teacher shows up consistently, students learn perseverance.

These lessons stay with students.

Additional Example: The Consistent Encourager

Ms. Ali was a high school biology teacher. She was not flashy or loud, but every test she returned included a handwritten note such as:

"I saw how hard you worked on this."

"You made real progress. Keep going."

"Your thinking here is strong. Well done."

Students began looking forward to her notes as much as their grades. She never sought attention, yet years later, many students described her as one of the best teachers they had ever known.

She led through presence, care, and consistency.

The Strength of Soft Power

Leading without being seen is a form of quiet strength. It is:

Influence without dominance

Authority without ego

Guidance without performance

This kind of leadership often looks like asking questions instead of giving every answer, inviting instead of ordering, and remaining steady even when no one notices.

It builds trust. It nurtures intrinsic motivation. It invites students to lead themselves.

When Leadership Feels Lonely

Leading quietly can sometimes feel lonely. When others are more visible or more publicly recognized, it is easy to wonder whether quiet leadership matters.

It does.

The teacher who listens more than they speak, who does not boast, and whose students feel safe without being spotlighted often leaves the deepest mark.

These are the teachers who change lives and never ask for credit.

Sustaining Quiet Leadership

To sustain this kind of leadership:

Celebrate small victories privately

Reflect on your impact through notes, journals, or feedback

Stay connected with likeminded colleagues

Protect time for renewal

Let your inner values guide you more than outside applause.

Reflective Takeaway

Leading without being seen is not about becoming invisible. It is about being intentional.

It means choosing to:

Build others instead of building your image

Shape lives instead of seeking attention

Do meaningful work even when no one is watching

You are the steady force behind student growth. You are the calm behind classroom stability. You are the quiet architect of confidence, hope, and learning.

You are the shepherd who does not need a spotlight because your light is reflected in the students you lift.

Keep leading. They are following, even when they do not yet realize it.

Reflection

Where do I lead quietly?

Am I comfortable influencing without recognition?

Research Anchor

Servant leadership strengthens trust and engagement within organizations (Greenleaf, 1977).

Chapter 13:
Knowing Them by Name

The Shepherd's Role

To someone unfamiliar with the flock, sheep may appear the same. But not to the shepherd. The shepherd knows each sheep by name, including its habits, history, patterns, and personality. They know which one startles easily, which one moves slowly, and which one tends to wander.

A name is more than a label. It represents relationship. It signals knowledge, connection, and care. When the shepherd calls, the sheep respond not only to the sound, but to the voice they trust.

Names matter because they communicate this truth: you are not just part of a group. You are seen as an individual.

The Teacher's Role

In the classroom, names carry meaning. When a teacher learns and uses a student's name with care and consistency, it communicates belonging, respect, and recognition.

Teachers who take time to learn, pronounce, and honor names are doing more than taking attendance. They are building trust and affirming identity. Students who feel known are more likely to participate, take risks, and believe they belong.

Knowing a student by name is often the first step toward knowing their story.

The Impact of Being Known

For some students, school may be the only place where their name is spoken with care. Being recognized is not simply about memory. It is about attention and respect. It means:

Remembering how they prefer to be addressed

Acknowledging nicknames or cultural pronunciation

Noticing shifts in tone or behavior

Students often connect being known with being valued. A simple greeting can shape the direction of a student's day.

Real Life Example: The Wall of Names

At a diverse middle school in Chicago, Mr. Patel created a first week tradition. Students shared the stories behind their names, including who gave them the name, what it meant, and how they felt about it. He then created a bulletin board called The Wall of Names.

The result was powerful. Students felt honored, and classmates developed a deeper respect for one another. Students even began gently correcting name mispronunciations themselves.

One student wrote, "This is the first time my name felt like a gift instead of a problem."

Names as the Beginning of Story

Every name carries history. When teachers invite students to share the meaning and background of their name, they create deeper connection.

Questions like these communicate care:

"Who chose your name?"

"Do you know what your name means?"

"Is there a name you would prefer I use?"

Knowing students by name opens the door to knowing them with greater depth.

Pronunciation as Respect

Repeatedly mispronouncing a student's name, especially after being corrected, can feel dismissive. It sends the message that the student's identity is not worth the effort.

Teachers who lead with respect:

Practice pronunciation

Invite corrections

Use phonetic guides when needed

This small effort communicates something significant. You matter enough for me to get this right.

Students should never feel that they must set aside their identity to be included.

Additional Example: The Name Card Strategy

Ms. Watson, a seventh grade teacher, used name tents during the first weeks of school. Each student wrote their name phonetically and included one fact about themselves.

She used the cards constantly and even practiced names at home. Within a few weeks, she could address every student with confidence and care.

Students later reported feeling more comfortable and more connected. One student said, "She is the first teacher who did not laugh after saying my name wrong."

Knowing names helped create belonging.

Beyond Names: Knowing the Whole Child

A name is the beginning, not the end, of being known. Teachers deepen relationships by:

Learning about interests and hobbies

Asking about family and community

Celebrating milestones and growth

Showing up at activities when possible

These actions remind students that they are more than grades or behavior. They are whole people.

When a Student Feels Forgotten

Every year, there are students who feel overlooked. They may sit quietly, complete their work, and avoid attention. They may not cause problems, but they may still feel unseen.

A single intentional interaction can change that. Saying a name with care, asking a thoughtful question, or recognizing an act of kindness can redirect a student's experience.

When Names Carry Pain

Some students carry names connected to painful memories, difficult relationships, or teasing. Others may be exploring identity and asking to be called by a different name.

Teachers who create safe spaces respond with respect and discretion. They ask:

"What name would you like me to use?"

"Is there anything you would like me to know?"

"Would you like support in communicating this to others?"

To know a student well is also to affirm who they are becoming.

Reflective Takeaway

Knowing students by name is more than a strategy. It is a philosophy.

It says:

You are not just one of many

You matter to me

I am paying attention

When students feel known, they are more likely to take academic risks, seek support, build connection, and believe they belong.

As a teacher, you are not simply calling roll. You are calling students into relationship.

And when they hear their name spoken with care, they begin to believe: I am seen. I am safe. I belong.

Keep learning their names, and keep showing them that they are more than names on a list.

Reflection

Do I pronounce every student's name correctly?

How do I honor identity in my classroom?

Research Anchor

A strong sense of belonging is closely connected to academic success (OECD, 2019).

Chapter 14: When the Flock Doubts the Path

The Shepherd's Role

Even with a trusted shepherd, there are moments when the flock resists moving forward. The path may feel unfamiliar. The ground may seem unstable. Fear may speak more loudly than trust.

In these moments, the shepherd does not force movement through pressure. They pause. They reassure. They walk the path first again. At times, they circle back, not because the path is wrong, but because the flock needs more time.

A wise shepherd understands that fear is not always rebellion. Often, it is uncertainty. And uncertainty responds better to calm than control.

The Teacher's Role

Students often question the direction you are leading them. They may resist assignments, challenge expectations, or shut down when the work feels unfamiliar or difficult. Often, what looks like defiance is actually doubt.

Students may be thinking:

Can I really do this?

What if I fail?

Why does this matter?

When students doubt the path, teachers can respond by demanding compliance or by deepening connection. The strongest teachers recognize the fear, build trust, and continue forward with patience.

Resistance is often rooted in fear, not laziness.

Building Trust Before Moving Forward

Before students will follow you into difficult learning, they need to trust you. Trust is built through:

Consistency in your presence and care

Clarity in explaining why the learning matters

Curiosity about how students are experiencing the journey

When a student says, "I do not get it," and the teacher responds with empathy rather than irritation, trust deepens.

Real Life Example: The Algebra Wall

Mr. Daniels taught eighth grade mathematics. In the middle of a unit on quadratic equations, his class hit a wall. Students became discouraged, participation dropped, and quiz scores declined.

Instead of forcing the pace, he paused. He told the class, "I can see this feels hard. Let us figure out how to move through it together."

He broke the learning into smaller steps, added visual activities, and let students choose review strategies.

By the end of the unit, performance improved, but more importantly, students felt heard and supported.

Mr. Daniels did not abandon the path. He adjusted it.

Recognizing Group Energy

Just as a flock can become uneasy together, classroom energy can shift quickly. One student's disengagement can spread, but so can one breakthrough.

Teachers read the room not only for behavior, but for emotion.

Signs that students may be doubting the path include:

Reduced participation

More off task behavior

Frequent complaints or avoidance

Repeated questioning of relevance

These moments do not mean failure. They signal the need for reconnection.

Strategies to respond include:

Revisiting the purpose of the learning

Offering meaningful choices

Celebrating small successes

When the Path Feels Unclear to the Teacher

There are also times when the teacher questions the path. The curriculum may feel disconnected. The goals may feel unrealistic. The pressure may feel heavy.

In those moments, honesty can build trust. A teacher can say:

"I am learning this with you."

"This part is challenging, but I believe we can work through it."

Authenticity creates connection. Connection creates momentum.

Additional Example: The Project Pivot

Ms. Rivera assigned a research project on historical speeches. Midway through the project, students became disengaged because the topics felt too distant from their interests.

She paused and asked, "What do you feel is missing?"

Students responded that they wanted speeches that felt relevant to their lives.

So she adjusted the project. Students were allowed to choose speeches from athletes, artists, and activists they admired.

Engagement returned. The work improved. The path did not fail. It needed to be realigned.

Empowering Student Voice

Students are more committed to learning when they believe their voice matters. Teachers can strengthen investment by:

Offering options in how students complete work

Gathering student feedback

Including students in classroom norms and expectations

This is not about losing control. It is about co-creating an experience worth trusting.

When students help shape the road, they are more willing to stay on it.

Holding the Vision

Teachers carry vision for students even when students cannot yet see it for themselves. A teacher's presence communicates:

This work is hard, but it matters

You may not see your growth yet, but I do

You are more capable than you realize

Students often borrow a teacher's belief until they develop their own.

Reflective Takeaway

When the flock doubts the path, the shepherd does not become louder.

They become closer. They slow down. They lead again with calm.

When students resist, they are often asking for reassurance.

Your steady presence in moments of uncertainty builds the bridge between fear and confidence.

You are the one who keeps believing, keeps adjusting, and keeps guiding forward, even when the path feels difficult.

Because the journey matters.

And so do they.

Reflection

How do I respond to student resistance?

Do I explain the purpose behind learning?

Research Anchor

Student autonomy is strongly connected to intrinsic motivation and engagement (Deci and Ryan, 2000).

Chapter 15: Guiding with Grace

The Shepherd's Role

Shepherds understand that movement does not happen perfectly. The flock does not always move in straight lines, and every sheep does not move at the same pace. Some get distracted. Some rush ahead. Others fall behind. Still, the shepherd remains patient and leads with grace.

Grace means recognizing that mistakes are part of movement, that growth is not always straight, and that correction can happen without shame. A shepherd redirects to restore, not to condemn.

The tone, pace, and touch of the shepherd reflect care. Discipline is offered with dignity. Redirection happens within relationship.

The Teacher's Role

In the classroom, guiding with grace means giving students room to learn and grow, even when they stumble. It means correcting behavior without damaging dignity. It means maintaining high expectations while offering support.

Grace is not about overlooking everything. It is about how teachers respond when students fall short.

When a student forgets an assignment, reacts poorly, or breaks a rule, grace says, let us use this moment for growth.

Balancing Accountability and Compassion

Strong teachers lead with both clarity and compassion. They hold students to meaningful expectations and help them reach those expectations.

Grace does not remove standards. It walks alongside students toward them.

This may sound like:

"You did not finish the project, but I will help you make a plan."

"Your tone was not respectful. Let us talk about what happened and how to move forward."

Students learn accountability not through shame, but through respectful correction and support.

Real Life Example: The Missed Deadline

In a high school English class, a student named Jordan missed an essay deadline for the third time. Ms. Palmer could have simply given a zero, but instead, she asked him to stay after class.

During their conversation, Jordan shared that he had been caring for younger siblings while his mother worked.

Ms. Palmer responded, "You still need to complete the assignment, but we can adjust the timeline, and I will help you stay on track."

Jordan turned in the essay a few days later. It was not perfect, but it was progress, and it came through trust rather than fear.

Grace made the expectation feel possible.

Creating a Culture of Second Chances

Classrooms shaped by grace:

Allow mistakes without permanent labels

Offer fresh starts

Value learning over punishment

This does not mean avoiding consequences. It means designing consequences that teach and restore.

For example:

A missed assignment may lead to reflection and revision

A behavior issue may lead to a restorative conversation

A conflict may become an opportunity to build empathy

When students know failure is not final, they are more willing to keep trying.

Modeling Grace Through Your Own Actions

Students learn grace by watching how teachers respond to their own mistakes and pressures. Teachers model grace when they:

Admit when they were wrong

Stay calm when plans fall apart

Extend patience during emotional moments

When a teacher says, "I made a mistake, and here is how I am going to make it right," students learn how to take responsibility without shame.

Additional Example: The Behavior Reset

In a third grade classroom, a student named Mia often interrupted lessons. Her teacher, Mr. Grant, recognized that her behavior was driven by anxiety rather than attention seeking.

Instead of removing her from the room, he created a quiet signal. When she felt overwhelmed, she could place a blue card on her desk and step away briefly to regulate herself.

The interruptions decreased. Mia felt respected and more in control.

Mr. Grant did not simply stop the behavior. He taught her how to manage it.

Grace and Equity

Grace is essential in equitable teaching because students come with different experiences, resources, and emotional capacities.

Guiding with grace may mean:

Being flexible with deadlines during crisis

Teaching concepts again without embarrassment

Providing multiple ways for students to demonstrate understanding

Fairness is not always sameness. Grace meets students where they are and helps them move forward.

Boundaries with Grace

Grace does not remove boundaries. It shapes how boundaries are delivered.

Teachers can:

Say no with kindness

Redirect with respect

Enforce rules with empathy

When students know that boundaries are rooted in care, they experience them as support rather than punishment.

Refilling the Well

Offering grace can be emotionally demanding, especially when teachers themselves feel drained.

To continue guiding with grace, teachers need to:

Practice self-compassion

Notice small moments of impact

Process with trusted colleagues

Create routines for rest and joy

Grace is a gift, and it must also be extended inward.

Reflective Takeaway

Guiding with grace is one of the most powerful ways a teacher can lead.

It tells students:

Your mistakes do not define you

You are worth the effort

Growth is still possible

Grace changes the culture of a classroom. It softens resistance and builds trust.

You are the one who helps students rise after they fall. You are the one who walks beside them with both strength and gentleness. You are the one who shows that correction and care belong together.

Keep guiding with firmness and compassion.

Grace is not weakness.

It is leadership at its finest.

Reflection

Do my corrections restore or shame?

How do I balance accountability and empathy?

Research Anchor

Shame reduces motivation, while compassion supports persistence and growth (Brown, 2012).

Part IV: The Journey and the Struggle

Chapter 16:
Crossing Difficult Terrain

The Shepherd's Role

Shepherds do not always lead their flock through green meadows and easy paths. Sometimes, the only way forward is through steep hills, rocky ground, or narrow passages. These routes test the flock's endurance, unity, and trust.

The shepherd moves carefully. At times, they carry the weakest. At other times, they stop so the flock can rest. Throughout the journey, they remain alert to danger. They do not pretend the path is easy. They prepare for its demands and lead through difficulty with confidence and care.

Crossing difficult terrain is not only about survival. It is also about growth.

The Teacher's Role

Teachers also guide students through difficult terrain. This may include challenging academic content, emotional struggles, personal hardships, or world events that weigh heavily on young minds. These seasons are not always smooth, and they are not always brief.

A teacher becomes a steady presence when students face adversity. Whether the challenge is a difficult unit in mathematics, a hard conversation about injustice, or a class processing shared grief, the teacher helps students continue moving forward.

Not by pretending everything is fine, but by walking beside them through the struggle.

Academic Struggles as Terrain

For many students, academic content can feel like a mountain. Concepts may not come easily. Learning differences and language barriers can make the climb even harder.

Teachers help students navigate this by:

Breaking learning into manageable steps

Celebrating progress as well as achievement

Teaching perseverance as a skill

Normalizing struggle as part of growth

When students hear, "This is hard, but I am here with you," they begin to build resilience.

Real Life Example: The Essay Marathon

Ms. Liu assigned a multi part essay to her tenth grade English class. Several students immediately felt overwhelmed and doubted they could complete it.

Instead of responding with pressure, she framed the essay as a journey. She told them, "We are climbing a writing mountain one step at a time."

Each day, students focused on one part of the process, including thesis statements, evidence, and transitions. She posted a visual trail map in the classroom so they could track their progress.

By the end of the assignment, nearly every student submitted a complete essay, and many had done so for the first time. Some even asked for the chance to revise their work.

Ms. Liu made the challenge feel possible and meaningful.

Emotional Terrain: When Life Interrupts Learning

Students bring their lives into the classroom. When they are dealing with divorce, food insecurity, anxiety, or grief, academic learning may no longer be their first concern.

Teachers can support students during these moments by:

Offering flexibility during emotionally heavy times

Providing space for reflection, journaling, or quiet work

Checking in with consistency and care

Helping students name their emotions

Crossing this kind of terrain often requires more listening than lecturing.

Sometimes the most important thing a teacher can offer is a calm and steady presence.

Social Terrain: Conflict and Belonging

School is also social terrain. Students face exclusion, misunder-standings, peer pressure, and relational tension.

Teachers support students by helping them:

Work through conflict with restorative dialogue

Build empathy and healthy boundaries

Reflect on behavior without shame

In these moments, teachers act as guides through the complex middle of social growth.

Sometimes the simple words, "I saw what happened. Let us work through it together," can give a student the direction they need.

Collective Terrain: Community and Global Crisis

There are seasons when the difficult terrain is shared by everyone. This may include:

A pandemic

Community violence

Natural disasters

Social or racial injustice

During these times, the classroom becomes a place for both learning and healing.

Teachers who lead well through collective struggle:

Make room for student voice

Address difficult realities with honesty and care

Offer hope alongside truth

Balance rigor with emotional responsiveness

You do not need to have every answer. You need to remain steady.

Additional Example: Teaching Through Tragedy

After a local shooting, Ms. Perez's high school students entered class withdrawn and unsettled. Rather than continuing with the day's lesson, she paused and asked, "What is on your mind today?"

Students shared fears, sadness, and confusion. Some cried. Others remained quiet. She listened, validated their emotions, and reminded them, "You are safe here, and we will walk through this together."

No academic content was covered that day, but something important still happened. Healing began.

Ms. Perez did not avoid the difficult terrain. She entered it with her students.

When the Teacher Is Also Tired

Crossing difficult terrain as a teacher can be exhausting. There are days when you are carrying students while also carrying your own burden.

In those moments, honesty matters. A teacher can say:

“I am having a hard day too, but I am still here.”

“Let us move through this slowly together.”

Support is also essential. Reach out to teammates, counselors, or administrators when needed.

You do not have to be a hero. You just have to keep walking.

Building Endurance for Hard Seasons

Students build strength for difficult moments when:

They are coached rather than criticized

They are allowed to struggle and supported through it

They reflect on what they have already overcome

Teachers can support this by including:

Reflection questions such as, “What was hard, and what helped?”

Class reminders such as, “We can do hard things.”

Stories of resilience from literature, history, and real life

This kind of endurance helps students approach future challenges with greater confidence.

Reflective Takeaway

Difficult terrain is not always a detour. Often, it is part of the journey.

Students may not remember every worksheet or assignment, but they will remember who stayed with them through the hardest parts.

You are their guide. You are their steady pace. You are the one who says, "This is hard, but I am not leaving."

Keep walking. The road may be steep, but you are not alone.

And neither are they.

Reflection

How do I respond during times of crisis?

Do I adjust my pace during hardship?

Research Anchor

Practices that build resilience contribute to stronger long term student achievement and well-being (Masten, 2014).

Chapter 17: Leaving the 99 for the One

The Shepherd's Role

Every shepherd understands this challenge. The flock may be large, but sometimes one sheep wanders away. It may be frightened, stuck, or simply separated from the others.

When that happens, a good shepherd does something bold. They leave the ninety-nine to go after the one.

This does not happen because the ninety-nine do not matter. It happens because each one matters deeply. The shepherd searches, climbs, calls out, and keeps going until the lost sheep is found. When they return, it is not with punishment. It is with relief and joy.

This is love that notices absence and chooses to respond.

The Teacher's Role

Teachers face the same choice. When a student falls behind, disengages, or disappears emotionally, the easier option is often to stay focused on the group and keep moving. There is always more curriculum to cover and more responsibilities to manage.

But the teacher who leads like a shepherd notices the absence. They feel it, and they respond.

They make the call. They send the message. They check in at lunch. They offer another chance.

Because every student matters, not only the high performing or well behaved, but especially the one who is drifting.

Recognizing Who Is Missing

Not every disappearance is physical. Sometimes a student is present in body but absent in spirit.

Signs that a student may be slipping away include:

Falling grades or reduced participation

Withdrawal from peers

Increased conflict or defiance

Loss of interest in things they once enjoyed

Teachers who know their students well notice these signs early and do not ignore them.

They say things like:

"I have noticed you seem different lately. Do you want to talk?"

"You used to really enjoy this. What has changed?"

"You matter in this class, and I have missed hearing from you."

Naming the absence is often the first act of rescue.

Real Life Example: The Missing Senior

Mr. Clay, a high school government teacher, had a senior named Devon who stopped coming to class just two weeks before graduation. He was technically passing, but only barely.

While others assumed he had given up, Mr. Clay made a different choice. He called home, contacted Devon's coach, and left a handwritten note at the front office that said, "Devon, I am rooting for you. Let us finish this together."

Devon returned quietly. Two weeks later, he crossed the graduation stage.

One student. One note. One more future reclaimed.

Making Time for the One

Reaching out to a struggling student requires time and emotional energy. But those moments can be the difference between disconnection and restoration.

It may look like:

Tutoring during lunch

A message sent through a school platform

A restorative conversation after class

A plan developed with a counselor or caregiver

These actions communicate one powerful truth: you are not forgotten.

Additional Example: The ESL Lifeline

In a middle school English as a second language class, Ms. Jaramillo had a student named Farid who had recently arrived from Syria. He was quiet, anxious, and academically behind.

One day, she stayed after school and brought in picture books written in Arabic. She asked him, “Will you help me pronounce these words?”

His eyes lit up. For the first time, he was the expert.

From that moment on, he began to smile more, participate more, and gain confidence in learning English.

She found the one by first honoring his strength.

Creating Systems of Rescue

Teachers who regularly notice and support the one often rely on intentional systems such as:

Tracking attendance and participation patterns

Using student feedback to check engagement

Building small group check ins or office hours

Creating low pressure ways for students to reconnect

This work should not be done alone. Teachers can collaborate with counselors, administrators, and colleagues to create stronger support systems.

Rescue is often a team effort.

Leading the Many While Reaching for One

Teachers may wonder whether focusing on one student will take too much away from the rest of the class.

Often, the opposite is true.

When students see their teacher go after the one, they learn something powerful:

No one is disposable

Everyone matters here

If I fall behind, someone will notice

This kind of care strengthens the entire classroom community.

When the One Does Not Return Right Away

Not every story resolves quickly. Sometimes the student does not respond. Sometimes the walls remain up.

Even then, the effort matters.

Students remember who tried. And sometimes, they come back later because someone left the door open.

Teachers can continue to offer hope by:

Writing a note they may not read immediately

Offering another chance even if it is not accepted right away

Saying, "When you are ready, I am still here."

Grace keeps the light on.

Reflective Takeaway

Leaving the ninety-nine for the one is not favoritism. It is faithfulness.

It communicates:

You are worth the effort

You are more than your behavior or your grade

I will not give up on you when things get hard

You are the one who notices absence and sees possibility. You are the one who calls students back with dignity. You are the one who carries the hurting home with compassion.

Keep noticing. Keep pursuing the one.

Because every student in your classroom is a story worth fighting for.

Reflection

Who needs my extra attention right now?

How do I pursue students who are disengaged?

Research Anchor

One strong relationship with a caring adult can significantly shape a student's life outcomes (Search Institute, 2018).

Chapter 18: The Shepherd's Staff

The Shepherd's Role

In the shepherd's hand is a staff, a tool of protection, guidance, and connection. It is more than a walking stick. It is a symbol of authority and care.

With it, the shepherd gently redirects sheep that are drifting off course. When danger appears, the staff becomes a means of defense. It serves as an extension of the shepherd's presence, a visible reminder of leadership and safety.

The staff is not used to create fear. It is held in trust. When sheep see the staff, they feel secure. They know they are not alone.

The Teacher's Role

For teachers, the staff takes many forms. It may be the classroom norms posted on the wall, the expectations that are taught and revisited, the steady tone used during tense moments, or the procedures that bring order and calm to the day.

A teacher's staff is not about control. It is about structure. It is the system of tools, routines, and boundaries that makes learning possible.

Without structure, confusion grows. With clear and consistent structure, students feel safe enough to learn, participate, and take risks.

Building a Culture of Consistent Expectations

Students thrive when they know what to expect. Consistency builds trust. Teachers lead with the staff when they:

Begin and end class with routines

Reinforce classroom values through daily practice

Hold all students to clear and fair expectations

Follow through with consequences that are consistent and respectful

The goal is not perfection. It is predictability.

Structure creates the safety students need in order to take academic, emotional, and social risks.

Real Life Example: The Morning Routine

Ms. Garcia, a sixth grade teacher, began every class the same way:

Greeting students by name at the door

Quiet entry and independent warm up

Review of the day's learning goal

Many of her students came from homes marked by unpredictability. Over time, they began arriving early. One student said, "I feel calm in this room."

The routine was simple, but it was dependable. It became the staff that grounded the class.

The Staff as a Symbol of Fairness

When rules are applied inconsistently, students lose trust. When expectations are carried out with fairness and dignity, students feel secure.

This kind of fairness may look like:

Addressing behavior privately instead of publicly

Allowing natural consequences without shame or sarcasm

Ensuring that every student has an opportunity to contribute and succeed

The staff protects. It does not punish for the sake of punishment.

Empowering Students to Carry the Staff

The strongest classrooms are shared spaces of responsibility. Teachers invite students to help uphold norms and care for the learning environment through:

Classroom roles that build ownership

Peer mediation or student leadership opportunities

Agreements created together at the beginning of the year

When students help carry the staff, they become more invested in the classroom community.

This is not about handing off discipline. It is about cultivating leadership.

Additional Example: Restorative Justice in Action

At Lincoln High School, Ms. Beck introduced restorative circles when conflict arose. Instead of assigning traditional detention, students participated in guided conversations focused on accountability, empathy, and repair.

Students discussed the impact of their actions and how to make things right.

One student reflected, "I did not just get punished. I felt understood."

In that classroom, the staff was not harsh. It was healing.

Practical Tools of the Staff

Teachers use many practical tools that function as the staff, including:

Nonverbal cues that redirect behavior quietly

Seating arrangements that reduce conflict

Calm down spaces for emotional regulation

Visual schedules that increase predictability

Clear rubrics and grading practices

Each tool communicates the same message: you are safe, you are supported, and we are in this together.

When the Staff Feels Heavy

At times, holding structure can feel exhausting. Repeating expectations, responding to behavior, and managing many personalities at once can wear a teacher down.

In those moments, remember:

It is okay to pause and reset

Expectations can be revisited at any point in the year

You do not have to carry everything alone

Rest is part of good leadership

The staff is not a burden. It is a gift. Still, even the shepherd needs rest.

Reflective Takeaway

The staff in your hand is more than a classroom management tool. It is a symbol of safety, a sign of care, and a structure that says, "In this room, we live and learn with purpose."

You lead not through force, but through consistency. Not through power, but through presence.

You are the one who creates a space where students know:

What is expected

What is possible

What is safe

You carry the staff. And with it, you help create a culture where students can thrive.

Keep holding it.

Keep leading with firmness, gentleness, and consistency.

Reflection

Are my expectations clear and consistent?

Do students experience boundaries as safety?

Research Anchor

Structured environments strengthen academic engagement and improve learning outcomes (Marzano, 2003).

Chapter 19:

Teaching in All Seasons

The Shepherd's Role

Shepherds do not work only when conditions are easy. They lead through every season, through the abundance of spring, the heat of summer, the change of autumn, and the hardship of winter. Each season brings different demands and requires different strengths.

In spring, there is new growth to nurture. In summer, there is work to sustain. In autumn, there is preparation for change. In winter, there is endurance and patience.

The shepherd shows up in every season, adapting, guiding, protecting, and persevering.

Because the flock still needs them, no matter the weather.

The Teacher's Role

Teaching is seasonal too. There are cycles of energy, focus, celebration, and exhaustion. There are seasons of momentum and seasons of discouragement. Great teachers understand that every season has a purpose.

Teachers do not simply respond to lesson plans. They respond to moods, maturity, stress, and shifting classroom dynamics. They learn to read the emotional weather of the room and adjust accordingly.

They continue showing up through the heat, the cold, and the unpredictability of school life because students need consistency in every season.

The Seasons of the School Year

Every school year carries its own rhythm:

Fall brings beginnings, routines, and relationship building

Winter often brings fatigue, deeper content, and emotional dips

Spring brings testing pressure, restlessness, and transition

The end of the year brings reflection, closure, and preparation for what comes next

Teachers who understand these rhythms prepare for them both emotionally and practically.

In fall, they build connection. In winter, they offer patience. In spring, they maintain structure. At the close of the year, they honor growth.

Each season matters. Each season brings both gifts and challenges.

Real Life Example: The Midyear Dip

Mr. Henderson, a middle school science teacher, noticed that every January his students returned from break tired, distracted, and disconnected.

Instead of pushing immediately into heavy content, he created a relaunch week. He revisited classroom norms, led team building activities, and introduced a fun science challenge using marsh-mallows and catapults.

The effect was immediate. Students laughed again. Participation increased. The spark returned.

Mr. Henderson did not resist the season. He responded to it wisely.

Emotional Seasons in Student Lives

Students move through personal seasons as well. A student may be navigating divorce, grief, loneliness, success, or change.

Teachers pay attention to these seasons. They:

Offer flexibility during hard times

Celebrate joyful moments

Create stability when life feels uncertain

This kind of seasonal awareness builds trust that lasts.

Sustaining Yourself in Every Season

Teachers also experience their own seasons of joy, frustration, burnout, renewal, and breakthrough.

To remain steady, it helps to:

Recognize your own rhythms and honor them

Build routines that include rest and renewal

Process hard days with trusted colleagues

Revisit notes or memories that remind you of your impact

You are not required to feel strong every day. Sometimes staying rooted is the victory.

Additional Example: The End of Year Reflection

At the end of each year, Ms. Doyle asked her fourth grade students to write letters to next year's class. They shared what helped them grow, what they loved, and what they wished new students would know.

When the new school year began, she read those letters aloud to her incoming class.

The ritual closed one season with gratitude and opened the next with hope.

It created continuity and reminded everyone that while seasons change, care remains.

Teaching Across Career Seasons

Beyond the school calendar, teachers also experience professional seasons:

The excitement of beginning

The confidence of experience

The wisdom of long term practice

Each season brings different strengths. What matters most is continuing to grow, adapt, and care.

Teachers may change roles, grade levels, or schools, but their influence deepens with each season of service.

When a Season Is Especially Hard

Some years are more difficult than others. There may be a challenging class dynamic, personal hardship, leadership changes, or ongoing stress.

In those moments:

Focus on what is within your control

Celebrate small wins

Seek guidance or mentorship

Remember that difficult seasons do pass

You are not stuck. You are moving through.

Reflective Takeaway

Every season matters.

The warm seasons build connection. The hard seasons deepen roots. The quiet seasons build endurance. The joyful seasons bring celebration.

You are the one who keeps showing up through calm and chaos, through sunshine and storm.

Because every child deserves a teacher who understands the rhythm of growth.

You are the one who:

Adjusts your pace without losing your direction

Shows up with grace in every condition

Leads with heart no matter what the season brings

Keep teaching in all seasons.

Your presence is part of the climate where students grow best.

Reflection

What season is my classroom in right now?

What season am I personally in?

Research Anchor

Teacher efficacy is strongly connected to student growth and achievement (Tschannen Moran, 2001).

Chapter 20: The Legacy of the Shepherd

The Shepherd's Role

When a shepherd leads day after day, guiding, protecting, nourishing, and seeking, something lasting is formed. Even after the sheep have moved on and the field has changed, the memory of the shepherd's presence remains.

The true impact of a shepherd is not always visible in the moment. It is revealed in the safety that was felt, the growth that took place, and the direction the flock continues to follow long after the shepherd is out of sight.

A shepherd's legacy is not built in one moment. It is built over time through consistency, compassion, and commitment.

The Teacher's Role

Teachers leave a legacy every day. It is seen in the way a student learns to trust, dares to speak, or begins to believe, "I can do this."

You may not see the full impact this week, this semester, or even this year. But your influence keeps moving outward into careers, families, communities, and futures.

Teachers shape lives, and those lives shape the world.

What Legacy Really Means

Legacy is not about fame. It is not about awards, plaques, or public praise. Legacy is about:

The students who still remember your voice years later

The adults who parent differently because of how you treated them as children

The leaders who think deeply because you made them feel safe to ask questions

The dreamers and creators who saw possibility because you reflected it back to them

You are part of stories you may never fully hear.

Real Life Example: The Reunion Thank You

At a twenty-five-year high school reunion, Ms. Rowe, a retired literature teacher, attended quietly, unsure whether anyone would remember her.

One by one, former students approached her and said things like:

"You told me I was a writer before I believed it."

"You taught me how to think, not just what to think."

"You were the only adult who noticed when I was hurting."

She cried, not because she had forgotten the work, but because she never realized how far it had echoed.

Teachers rarely receive standing ovations. But their influence lives on in homes, workplaces, and classrooms everywhere.

Creating a Legacy Intentionally

You do not have to wait decades to know that you are building a legacy. It is happening whenever you:

Greet students by name with warmth

Connect lessons to real life

Show up with integrity on hard days

Apologize when you are wrong

Celebrate effort as well as success

Every interaction is a seed. You may not see it grow, but it is growing.

Legacy in the Quietest Moments

Big moments matter, but legacy also lives in small ones:

A hallway conversation

A note placed on a desk

Extra help after school

A moment of listening when a student felt unseen

So much of a teacher's legacy is carried in quiet statements like:

"Because of you, I kept going."

"Because of you, I believed I could."

Additional Example: The Handwritten Letter

Each year, Mr. Owens wrote a personal letter to every graduating senior in his government class. Each letter was short, thoughtful, and handwritten.

He wrote things like, "I see this strength in you," "I am proud of your growth," and "Do not forget what you are capable of."

Years later, many former students still kept those letters.

His legacy was not simply in what he taught. It was in how he made students feel remembered.

Leaving a Legacy with Colleagues

Teachers also shape the adults around them. Legacy lives in:

The mentor who helps a new teacher survive the first year

The colleague who shares resources generously

The veteran educator who models calm and grace under pressure

Your legacy is not only with students. It is also in the culture you help build among adults.

Be the reason someone stays in education. Be the voice that reminds another teacher that they are making a difference.

When You Wonder Whether It Matters

Some days, it is easy to ask:

Is anyone listening?

Am I really making a difference?

You are.

Every note, lesson, kind word, correction, and act of care creates ripples you may never fully see.

You are not just teaching content. You are teaching courage, compassion, and perseverance.

And those lessons last.

Reflective Takeaway

A teacher's legacy is not built in one school year. It is built in the daily decision to care, to keep trying, and to believe in what is possible even when the work is hard.

You are the shepherd, and your flock remembers.

Maybe not immediately. Maybe not until years later. But when students look back, they will remember the steady presence that helped shape who they became.

Keep showing up. Keep leading with heart. Keep planting seeds.

The field may keep changing, but your legacy endures.

And generations will walk paths made clearer because you walked them first.

Reflection

What do I hope students remember about me?

What am I modeling each day?

Research Anchor

Teachers have measurable long-term effects on student earnings and life outcomes (Chetty, Friedman, and Rockoff, 2014).

Part V: The Framework

The Shepherd Leadership Framework

A Practical Model for Schools and Districts

The twenty chapters of this book align with five foundational pillars of shepherd leadership.

Pillar 1: Presence

Chapters 1, 8, 11, and 12
Leadership begins with showing up consistently and intentionally.

Pillar 2: Protection

Chapters 3, 5, 9, and 18
Students thrive when safety, structure, and dignity are secure.

Pillar 3: Pursuit

Chapters 7 and 17
No student is invisible. Intervention must be intentional.

Pillar 4: Provision

Chapters 2, 6, and 13
Students must be known and nourished academically and emotionally.

Pillar 5: Persistence

Chapters 4, 14, 15, 16, 19, and 20
Leadership endures through seasons, setbacks, and uncertainty.

Conclusion: The Sacred Weight of the Work

You have walked the field.
You have held the staff.
You have noticed the one.
You have taught in every season.

This book has never truly been about sheep and pastures. It has always been about people. It has been about classrooms. It has been about the unseen, often unrecognized, yet unforgettable work of being a teacher.

You do not just teach.

You lead.
You protect.
You pursue.
You believe.

You believe on the easy days, and even more importantly, on the hard ones.

Every hallway you have walked.
Every desk you have straightened after the bell.
Every parent message you have answered with patience.
Every student you have looked in the eye and told, "You matter."

It all echoes.

Because the truth is, this work is not only instructional. It is deeply human. It is deeply meaningful. It calls on your voice, your energy, your patience, and your heart. It asks you to keep planting seeds even when the soil feels dry. It asks you to keep showing up when the flock resists. It asks you to keep leading when the path is uncertain.

And still, you do it.

Not because it is easy.
But because you understand the sacred weight of the work.

You are a shepherd in sneakers.
A guardian of potential.
A quiet architect of futures.

You walk ahead not for applause and not for recognition, but because you know that behind you is a generation that needs direction, stability, and belief.

Your classroom is not just a room.

It is a pasture of possibility.
A training ground for courage.
A shelter from storms.
A bridge to becoming.

And you, yes you, are the one who helps make it possible.

So when the days feel long, when the system feels broken, and when the burden feels too heavy, return to this truth:

You are not just leading a class.
You are shaping a legacy.

One life at a time.
One name at a time.
One rescued student at a time.

Thank you for being the shepherd.

The field is better because you are in it.
And the world will be better because of the lives you have led.

Author's Note

Writing this book has been a labor of deep gratitude.

As an educator and speaker, I have met teachers from every walk of life, some seasoned and some just beginning, all carrying the same hope: to make a difference.

What I have learned is this. Being a teacher is not just a job. It is a calling. It is the courageous act of leading others, often without a map, often without recognition, but always with heart.

This book draws inspiration from the ancient role of the shepherd because that image captures the quiet strength, relentless care, and humble leadership required of teachers today.

Thank you for picking up this book. More importantly, thank you for picking up your staff every morning and stepping into the lives of students who need your guidance.

You are seen.
You are valued.
You are changing the world.

Keep leading.
Keep loving.
Keep showing up.

With respect and admiration,

Dennard Mitchell

www.ingramcontent.com/pod-product-compliance
Lightning Source LLC
LaVergne TN
LVHW090528110826
845146LV00003B/1028

* 9 7 9 8 2 3 4 0 6 7 6 4 7 *